PARAGUAY 2016 HUMAN RIGHTS REPORT

EXECUTIVE SUMMARY

Paraguay is a multiparty, constitutional republic. In April 2013, Horacio Cartes of the Colorado Party, also known as the National Republican Association, won the presidency in elections recognized as free and fair.

During the period covered by this report, civilian authorities maintained effective control over the security forces. Critics, however, asserted the government did not deploy or monitor forces effectively, particularly in the northeastern section of the country.

The principal human rights problems were generalized impunity and corruption, particularly among the judiciary and law enforcement; harsh and at times life-threatening prison conditions; and police involvement in criminal activities.

Other human rights problems included lengthy pretrial detention and trial delays; the intimidation of journalists by organized-crime groups and government officials; lack of access to land for the rural poor; discrimination and violence against women, indigenous persons, persons with disabilities, and lesbian, gay, bisexual, transgender, and intersex (LGBTI) persons; and trafficking in persons. Incidents of child labor and violations of worker rights were reported with some regularity.

The executive branch took steps to prosecute and punish officials who committed abuses, but general impunity for officials in the police and security forces continued to be widely reported.

Section 1. Respect for the Integrity of the Person, Including Freedom from:

a. Arbitrary Deprivation of Life and other Unlawful or Politically Motivated Killings

There were several reports that the government or its agents committed arbitrary or unlawful killings.

On June 19, the Attorney General's Office ordered the arrest of nine agents of Paraguay's National Antinarcotics Secretariat (SENAD) for a failed operation on June 18 that resulted in the death of a three-year-old girl by gunshot. The incident occurred in Nueva Italia, Central Department, in full view of civilian witnesses

who alleged the SENAD agents did not identify themselves or attempt to verify the identity of the civilians before firing more than 60 bullets at them. The Attorney General's Office charged the agents with murder and attempted murder. The case was pending as of November 1.

On April 30, the Attorney General's Office ordered the arrest of three San Pedro Department Councilmen, charging them with aggravated murder for the April 24 death of Ramon Carillo, the mayor of Tacuati. The case was pending as of November 1.

Armed guerrilla groups continued to target and kill security forces. During the year, the Paraguayan government alleged the Paraguayan People's Army (EPP) killed eight military personnel and kidnapped three civilians. The kidnapping victims remained missing as of November 1.

Incidents of violence related to narco-trafficking were prevalent in the northeastern region. On June 16, unidentified assailants gunned down prominent narco-trafficker Jorge Rafaat on one of the major thoroughfares in the city of Pedro Juan Caballero. On August 5, assassins shot and killed Miguel Louteiro Echeverría, the mayor of Bella Vista Norte, Amambay, and his secretary Celso Carballo, shortly after a large police seizure of cocaine. On August 9, two assailants on a motorcycle shot and killed police officer Osvaldo Ramirez Lezcano in Curuguaty, Canindeyu Department.

On July 11, a Paraguayan court convicted all 11 defendants involved in the 2012 Marina Cue confrontation near Curuguaty that resulted in the death of 11 protestors and six police officers. In a ruling of more than 2,000 pages, four defendants received four years, or time served, for criminal association; three defendants received six years, including two under house arrest, for complicity to murder, criminal association, and land invasion; and, four defendants were sentenced to between 18 and 35 years for land invasion, criminal association, and attempted premeditated murder. Defense attorneys appealed the sentence on August 1, and the appeal was pending as of November 1.

On July 24, defense attorneys and Amnesty International filed a complaint with the Attorney General's Office alleging security forces tortured several of the Marina Cue protestors and killed two of them. The court that convicted the 11 defendants recommended that the Attorney General's office investigate these allegations, but the Attorney General's office has not announced an investigation or made findings available to the public. On October 26, Senate President Roberto Acevedo announced the formation of an independent commission led by Diego Bertolucci to investigate the role of the police in the events of June 15, 2012, in Curuguaty/Marina Cue.

b. Disappearance

There were no reports of politically motivated disappearances. There were press and government reports of short-term "express kidnappings" for monetary gain, particularly in the departments of San Pedro and Concepcion.

The Special Human Rights Unit in the Attorney General's Office investigated two cases of forced disappearance, compared with 25 cases in 2015, and investigated five cases of kidnapping.

On June 23, the Attorney General's Office charged and ordered the arrest of police officers for aggravated assault and kidnapping of Juan Marcos Rivera Dominguez in San Lorenzo. Rivera was later released without paying a ransom. The case was pending as of November 1.

On July 27, the EPP kidnapped Franz Wiebe Boschman, a farmer from San Pedro Department, and demanded a $700,000 ransom, but Wiebe's family was unable to pay. The government alleged the EPP or an offshoot organization kidnapped rancher Felix Urbieta on October 12 in Concepcion Department. Additionally, the government alleged the EPP still held Eladio Edelio Morinigo, a police officer, and Abraham Fehr, a Paraguayan-Mexican dual national farmer, both of whom the EPP kidnapped in 2014 and 2015, respectively. Morinigo's, Fehr's, Wiebe's, and Urbieta's whereabouts and conditions were unknown as of November 1.

c. Torture and Other Cruel, Inhuman, or Degrading Treatment or Punishment

The law prohibits such practices, and the government generally respected these provisions, but there were credible reports that some government officials employed such practices. The Attorney General's Human Rights Unit opened 31 torture investigation cases during the year, but there were no convictions, and all investigations were pending at the end of the year. Unlike criminal cases not involving torture, torture charges do not have a statute of limitations nor a defined period within which charges, an investigation, or the oral trial must be completed.

Several civil society groups publicly criticized the Joint Task Force (FTC), which operates in northeastern Paraguay and includes personnel from the armed forces, the National Police, and SENAD, for human rights violations in the northeastern region of the country. Five bishops issued a letter denouncing the Attorney General's Office and the tactics used by the FTC against the local population as abusive and arbitrary violations of human rights.

On August 17, Diana Vargas, commissioner of the independent government watchdog agency the National Mechanism to Prevent Torture (NMPT), filed a formal complaint with the Attorney General's Office alleging that police officers in the city of Ciudad del Este tortured a detainee. Vargas claimed doctors in the regional hospital had detected evidence of torture, but did not alert authorities. The case was pending as of November 1.

Prison and Detention Center Conditions

Prison and detention center conditions continued to fall short of international standards. Conditions were harsh and, at times, potentially life threatening due to inmate violence, mistreatment, overcrowding, poorly trained staff, deteriorating infrastructure, and unsanitary living conditions.

Physical Conditions: According to a report by NMPT in June, the country's 16 penitentiaries held almost double their design capacity. The NMPT also reported that nine facilities for juveniles housed 21 percent more inmates than their design capacity. Penitentiaries did not have adequate accommodations for inmates with physical disabilities.

The Justice Ministry's Directorate for the Care of Convicted Juveniles assigned minors convicted of juvenile crimes to one of nine youth correctional facilities in the country, one of which was dedicated to young women. Some juvenile offenders served their sentences in separate sections of adult prisons, such as the women's Ciudad del Este penitentiary.

According to official reports, 42 prisoners died in custody during the year: 18 from natural causes/illnesses, ten from inmate-on-inmate violence, six from smoke inhalation caused by the prison fire in Tacumbu, two from accidental electrocutions, one during a riot, one from suicide, and four from undefined causes.

There were credible reports that criminal rings engaged in extortion and racketeering within the country's prisons.

Prisons lacked adequate security controls and prison guard staffing, especially at Tacumbu prison. Inmates were frequently caught carrying handmade weapons, and there were reports of inmates committing acts of violence, including rape, against other inmates. There were four prison riots during the year resulting in injuries to prison guards and inmates, two inmate deaths, and extensive property damage.

Prisons and juvenile facilities generally lacked adequate temperature control systems, of particular concern during the exceedingly hot summer months. Some prisons had cells with inadequate lighting, in which prisoners were confined for long periods without an opportunity for exercise. Although sanitation and medical care were generally considered adequate, some prisons lacked sufficient medical personnel. Adherence to fire prevention norms was lacking.

On June 10, an electrical short-circuit in a basement workshop caused a fire in Tacumbu prison. Six inmates and the prison Security Chief, Blas Gaona, were killed, while ten inmates suffered from smoke inhalation and burns. Gaona died while freeing several trapped prisoners. The Attorney General's Office opened an investigation of possible negligence that may havecaused the fire and the government's response, and the investigation was ongoing as of November 1.

Administration: Visitors reportedly needed to offer bribes to visit prisoners, hindering effective representation of inmates by public defenders. During the year, the Justice Ministry's Internal Affairs Office continued random, unannounced visits to several prisons. Although married and unmarried heterosexual inmates were permitted conjugal visits, the Justice Ministry prohibited such visits for homosexual inmates.

Independent Monitoring: The government granted the media, independent civil society groups, and diplomatic representatives access to prisons with prior coordination. Representatives of the media, UNCAT, the ombudsman's office, and NGOs conducted regular prison visits. Government agencies, such as the NMPT, the Public Defender's office, and representatives of the Judicial Branch also conducted independent visits. By law, the Judicial Branch is responsible for overseeing funds it transfers annually to the Justice Ministry.

d. Arbitrary Arrest or Detention

The law prohibits arbitrary arrest and detention, but the government did not always observe these prohibitions. The law stipulates that persons detained without a judge-ordered arrest warrant must appear before a judge within 24 hours for an initial hearing. Police may arrest a person apprehended in the act of committing a crime and detain the suspect for up to six hours, after which the Attorney General's Office may detain persons up to 24 hours. In some cases, police ignored requirements for a warrant by citing obsolete provisions that allow detention if individuals are unable to present personal identification upon demand (although the law does not obligate citizens to carry or show identity documentation).

On May 25, Santiago Ortiz, the Secretary General of the Union of Paraguayan Journalists, filed a complaint with the Attorney General's Office alleging a group of police officers detained and physically assaulted him. The police stated they detained Ortiz after he refused to produce his personal identification. The case was still pending as of November 1.

Role of the Police and Security Apparatus

The National Police, under the authority of the Interior Ministry, are responsible for preserving public order, protecting the rights and safety of persons and entities and their property, preventing and investigating crimes, and implementing orders given by the judiciary and public officials. The constitution charges military forces with guarding the country's territory and borders. By law civilian authorities are in charge of the security forces.

The law authorizes the president to mobilize military forces domestically against any "internal aggression" endangering the country's sovereignty, independence, or the integrity of its democratic constitutional order. The law requires the president to notify congress within 48 hours of a decision to deploy troops. By law the president's deployment order must define geographic location, be subject to congressional scrutiny, and have a set time limit. As of September 12, a total of 310 personnel from the FTC were deployed to the departments of Concepcion, San Pedro, and Amambay in accordance with the law to allow military mobilization domestically.

The Defense Ministry, also under the president's authority but outside the military's chain of command, handles some defense matters. The ministry is responsible for the logistical and administrative aspects of the armed forces, especially the development of defense policy.

The law authorizes the SENAD and the National Police's Anti-Narcotics Unit, both under the president's authority, to enforce the law in matters related to narcotics trafficking and terrorism, respectively. The law provides for SENAD to lead operations in coordination with the Attorney General's Office and judiciary. To arrest individuals or use force, SENAD must involve members of the National Police in its operations, but it reportedly often did not do so.

The Human Rights Unit of the Attorney General's Office and the Disciplinary Review Board of the National Police are responsible for determining whether police killings legitimately occurred in the line of duty. The military justice system has jurisdiction over active military personnel.

On July 23, inmates detained in the Vinas Cue military prison contested their incarceration by claiming the government never published in the official government registry the military laws under which they were being held. Defense lawyers and family members allege that 90 percent of those sentenced or held without trial were arrested in retribution for whistleblowing on corruption cases involving high ranking officials.

On March 2, the president ordered the transfer and investigation of six officers accused of physically and psychologically abusing several underage cadets at a military school in Central Department. The case was pending as of November 1.

The Special Human Rights Unit in the Attorney General's office investigated 182 cases of excessive use of force by security forces, opened 31 cases of torture, investigated 52 cases of improper prosecution of innocents, and investigated seven cases of improper conviction of innocents. No information was available as to whether any of these cases resulted in convictions or penalties.

Although the National Police reportedly struggled with inadequate training, funding, and widespread corruption, it continued to investigate and punish members involved in crimes and administrative violations. On July 12, the National Police removed 14 police chiefs from Canindeyu Department after uncovering evidence they received bribes to allow the transport of approximately 20 tons of marijuana.

Several human rights NGOs and the media reported incidents of police involvement in homicides, rape, arms and narcotics trafficking, car theft, robbery, extortion, and kidnapping, with reported abuses particularly widespread in Ciudad del Este and other locations on the border with Brazil.

On August 18, a court sentenced three police officers to 18 years in prison and a fourth to four years in prison for their involvement in a 2012 robbery of 5.2 billion Guaranies (Gs.) ($945,400) from a security firm.

Arrest Procedures and Treatment of Detainees

Police may arrest individuals with a warrant or with reasonable cause. The law provides that after making an arrest, police have up to six hours to notify the Attorney General's office, at which time that office has up to 24 hours to notify a judge if it intends to prosecute. The law allows judges to use measures such as house arrest and bail in felony cases. According to civil society representatives and legal experts, in misdemeanor cases judges frequently set bail too high for many poor defendants to post bond, while they set minimal or no bail for the wealthy or for those with political connections.

The law grants defendants the right to hire counsel, and the government provides public defenders for those who cannot afford counsel. According to the NGO Paraguayan Human Rights Coordinator (CODEHUPY), heavy caseloads adversely affected the quality of representation by public defenders. Detainees had access to family members.

Arbitrary Arrests: The law prohibits arbitrary arrest and detention. CODEHUPY reported several cases during the year of arbitrary arrest and detention of persons without a warrant.

On January 20, four residents of Hernandarias, Alto Parana Department, filed a formal complaint alleging two police officers and two other unidentified individuals detained them as robbery suspects, tortured them, and threatened to kill them on January 8. They also filed a complaint against Prosecutor Humberto Rossetti as an accomplice for being present during the alleged torture. The allegations included the use of electric cattle prods, beatings, and asphyxiation with nylon bags. The case was pending as of November 1.

Pretrial Detention: The law permits detention without trial for a period equivalent to the minimum sentence associated with the alleged crime, a period that could range from six months to five years. Some detainees were held in pretrial detention beyond the maximum allowed time.

<u>Detainee's Ability to Challenge Lawfulness of Detention before a Court</u>: The law provides detainees with the right to prompt judicial review of the legality of their detention. Defendants have the right to initiate habeas corpus, habeas data, and other court proceedings to decide the lawfulness of detention or otherwise obtain a court-ordered release. Defendants have the right to sue the state for unlawful detention.

e. Denial of Fair Public Trial

The constitution provides for an independent judiciary. Undue external influence, however, often compromised the judiciary's independence. Interested parties, often including politicians, routinely attempted to influence investigations and pressure judges and prosecutors. Judicial selection and disciplinary review board processes were often politicized, with specific seats on the board allocated by law to congressional representatives, presidential nominees, lawyer's union representatives, law professors, and Supreme Court justices.

The Council of Magistrates (CEM) continued to utilize a process to improve transparency in selecting judges. The process filtered out a number of unsuitable candidates during the year.

Courts were inefficient and subject to corruption, and allegations that some judges and prosecutors solicited or received bribes to drop or modify charges against defendants were reported. Authorities generally respected court orders.

Trial Procedures

The constitution provides for the right to a fair public trial, which the judiciary nominally provides, albeit through a lengthy trial process.

Defendants enjoy a presumption of innocence and a right of appeal. Both defendants and prosecutors may present written testimony from witnesses and other evidence. Defendants have the right of access to state evidence relevant to their cases and may confront adverse witnesses, except in cases involving domestic or international trafficking in persons, in which case victims may testify remotely or in the presence of the defendant's lawyers, in lieu of the defendant. Defendants have the right to prompt information and detail of the indictments and charges they face, but some defendants received notification only when they faced arrest charges or seizure of their property.

Defendants have the right to access free interpretation services from the moment they are charged through all appeals, including translation to Guarani--the country's second official language. Defendants have the right to a fair trial without undue delay as well as the right to be present at the trial. Defendants have the right to communicate with an attorney of their choice or one provided at public expense. Defendants have the right to a reasonable amount of time to prepare their defense and to access their legal files and government-held evidence. Defendants may confront prosecution or plaintiff witnesses and present their own witnesses and evidence. Defendants are not compelled to testify or confess guilt and may choose to remain silent.

The Special Human Rights Unit in the Attorney General's Office investigated four cases of security forces using psychological and physical pressure to obtain statements from citizens during the year.

Political Prisoners and Detainees

There were no reports of political prisoners or detainees.

Civil Judicial Procedures and Remedies

Citizens have access to the courts to file lawsuits seeking damages for, or cessation of, human rights violations. There are administrative and judicial remedies for alleged wrongs, and authorities generally granted them to citizens. The court may order civil remedies, including fair compensation to the injured party; however, the government has experienced problems enforcing court orders in such cases. Individuals and organizations may appeal adverse domestic decisions to regional human rights bodies.

Property Restitution

The government generally enforced court orders with respect to seizure, restitution, or compensation for taking private property. Systemic inadequacies within the land registry system, however, prevented the government from compiling a reliable inventory of its landholdings. Registered land far exceeded the size of the country, and there were allegations of corruption within local government and INDERT, the government agency charged with registering and administering land, and reports of forced evictions.

On October 8, approximately 1,200 police personnel used a water cannon and rubber bullets to evict approximately 200 campesino families on disputed land in Colonia Guahory, Caaguazu Department. Currently, 70 Brazilian-Paraguayan families claim title to the 2,200 hectares of land, alleging the campesino families began occupying 1,200 hectares of it in 2014 and have been renting it to local and national political figures. The Brazilian-Paraguayan families admitted to paying the police Gs. 200 million ($36,364) to proceed with the operation. Police also initiated an eviction operation on September 15 in which they allegedly demolished and burned numerous informal structures belonging to the campesino families. Legal counsel for the campesino families alleged the Brazilian-Paraguayan families illegally purchased land titles. The case was pending as of November 1.

On April 4, Vilmar and Joel Eisen recovered their property after being illegally evicted in 2014 in a process initiated by the mayor of San Carlos del Apa, Concepcion Department.

Despite the government's acceptance of the donation of the disputed land on which the June 2012 Marina Cue confrontation occurred, the Public Registry did not transfer or register the property. Officials explained they could not act until lawsuits establishing previous ownership were resolved.

The registered land far exceeded the size of the country and there were credible allegations of the complicity of judges and public officials in falsifying land titles for the purpose of usurping property from legitimate owners.

f. Arbitrary or Unlawful Interference with Privacy, Family, Home, or Correspondence

The constitution and law prohibit such actions, and the government generally respected these prohibitions, but there were reports that members of the security forces failed to respect the law in certain instances. CODEHUPY, local Catholic Church organizations, and some national legislators alleged FTC personnel in the departments of Concepcion, San Pedro, and Amambay searched homes and schools without warrants. The Special Human Rights Unit in the Attorney General's Office investigated seven cases of unlawful interference with private correspondence during the year.

On August 25, newspaper *ABC Color* alleged that General Luiz Gonzaga Garcete, Commander of the Paraguayan Armed Forces, ordered two military intelligence units to spy on an *ABC Color* journalist who had been investigating an alleged corruption scandal involving Garcete and his wife. The allegations were under investigation by the Attorney General's Office as of November 1.

Section 2. Respect for Civil Liberties, Including:

a. Freedom of Speech and Press

The law and constitution provide for freedom of speech and press, and the government generally respected these rights. An independent press, an effective judiciary, and a functioning democratic political system combined to promote freedom of speech and press.

Violence and Harassment: Journalists occasionally suffered harassment, intimidation, and violence, primarily from drug-trafficking gangs and criminal groups but also from politicians and police. The media and international NGOs reported several such incidents against journalists.

On January 9, Brazilian authorities arrested Flavio Acosta Riveros, accused of murdering *ABC Color* journalist Pablo Medina and his assistant Antonia Chaparro in 2014. On February 27, authorities requested his extradition from Brazil, which is still pending with Brazilian authorities. Vilmar "Neneco" Acosta, former Mayor of Ypehu, is in prison awaiting trial for ordering the assassination of Medina and Chaparro. Authorities continued to search for Wilson Acosta Marques, whom they accused of participating in the assassination. The case was pending as of November 1.

Libel/Slander Laws: Politicians sometimes responded to media criticism by invoking criminal libel and slander laws and suing the media to intimidate journalists and suppress further investigations. Defamation is punishable by imprisonment for up to three years and significant fines.

Internet Freedom

The government did not restrict or disrupt access to the internet or censor online content, and there were no credible reports the government monitored private online communications without appropriate legal authority.

The International Telecommunication Union (ITU) reported 44 percent of inhabitants used the internet in 2015. This did not reflect the existing and growing number of individuals who had access to the internet at work or through mobile phones. According to the ITU, there were 105 cell phones for every 100 citizens.

Academic Freedom and Cultural Events

There were no government restrictions on academic freedom or cultural events.

b. Freedom of Peaceful Assembly and Association

The law provides for the freedoms of assembly and association, and the government generally respected these rights.

c. Freedom of Religion

See the Department of State's *International Religious Freedom Report* at www.state.gov/religiousfreedomereport/.

d. Freedom of Movement, Internally Displaced Persons, Protection of Refugees, and Stateless Persons

The law provides for freedom of internal movement, foreign travel, emigration, and repatriation, and the government generally respected these rights. The government's National Commission of Refugees cooperated with the Office of the UN High Commissioner for Refugees (UNHCR) and other humanitarian organizations in providing protection and assistance to internally displaced persons, refugees, returning refugees, asylum seekers, stateless persons, and other persons of concern. The NGO Committee of Churches for Emergency Aid acted as the local legal representative of the UNHCR.

Foreign Travel: By law, authorities may deny the issuance of passports to citizens who do not show proof they have met their tax obligations.

Protection of Refugees

Access to Asylum: The country's laws provide for the granting of asylum or refugee status, and the government has established a system for providing protection to refugees.

<u>Durable Solutions</u>: The government has provisions for integration, resettlement, and return of refugees. UNHCR reports that at the end of 2015, there were 209 total persons of concern present in country; 172 refugees and 37 asylum-seekers. Authorities permitted persons whose asylum or refugee status cases were refused to seek other migration options, including obtaining legal permanent residency in the country or returning to the most recent point of embarkation. The government did not assist in the safe, voluntary return of refugees to their homes, but rather relied on UNHCR assistance to facilitate such returns.

Section 3. Freedom to Participate in the Political Process

The constitution and laws provide citizens the ability to choose their government in free and fair periodic elections held by secret ballot and based on universal and equal suffrage.

Elections and Political Participation

<u>Recent Elections</u>: In November 2015, the country held nationwide multiparty municipal elections with international observers from the Organization of American States (OAS), Union of South American Nations, and Inter-American Union of Electoral Organizations. The OAS characterized the elections as free and fair. Observers noted several shortcomings, however, including the weakness of campaign financing regulations.

<u>Political Parties and Political Participation</u>: The National Republican Association Party and the Liberal Party maintained long-standing control of the political process. The parties politicized the Supreme Court, lower courts, and the selection and disciplining of judges and prosecutors.

New, small, and nontraditional political parties faced hurdles in securing sizable congressional representation due to seat allocation formulas in the electoral code, which favor larger parties.

The electoral code allows voters to select slates of candidates (that are drawn up by party leaders) rather than individual candidates. Candidates running for executive office, such as for president, mayor, and governor, run on individual ballots. Independent candidates face obstacles in setting up and running campaigns, since by law they must form a movement or political party and present a minimum number of candidates in a slate in order to compete.

<u>Participation of Women and Minorities</u>: The electoral code requires that at least 20 percent of each party's candidates in internal party primaries be women, and parties followed the requirement. Women served in both the legislature and the Supreme Court. There were 21 women in congress (nine of 45 senators and 12 of 80 national deputies, or 17 percent).

Although there were no legal impediments to participation by minorities or indigenous persons in government, no individuals from those groups served as a governor or in the cabinet, legislature, or Supreme Court.

Section 4. Corruption and Lack of Transparency in Government

The law provides criminal penalties for corruption by officials, but the government generally did not implement the law effectively. Corruption in all branches and at all levels of government remained widespread, with hundreds of cases of embezzlement, tax evasion, falsified documents, and criminal association. Cases typically spent several years in the courts. Under a law that prohibits court cases from lasting longer than four years, politicians and influential individuals convicted in lower courts routinely avoided punishment by filing appeals and motions until reaching the statute of limitation. Although indictments and convictions for corruption of low- and mid-level public officials occur with regularity, high-ranking public officials enjoy a high degree of impunity. Sometimes such officials are forced to resign or are indicted, but formal complaints rarely lead to convictions.

<u>Corruption</u>: On July 7, the Economic Crimes and Corruption Unit of the Attorney General's Office opened an investigation into the Chief of Defense, Luis Gonzaga Garcete, and his wife, Lucia Duarte de Garcete, for fraud and abuse of authority associated with the misuse of approximately Gs. 38.5 billion ($7 million) of public funds. On August 19, the Attorney General's Office transferred the investigation to the Supreme Court of Military Justice due to jurisdiction concerns. No charges were filed and the investigation was pending as of November 1.

On June 21, a Paraguayan court of appeals upheld sentences handed down December 15, 2015, against 12 executive directors and board members of the Itaipu Pension Fund for the breach of trust and fraud involving $48 million. The court sentenced Victor Bogado Nunez and Mariano Escurra Vicesar to 14 years in prison; Felix Villamayor, Cesar Bejarano, and Walter Delgado to 12 years; Ricardo Antonio Perreira Polleti to 10 years; Jose Szwako, Jose Alonso, and Pabla Mieres to eight years; Cibar Insfran to four years; and, Gustavo Dure Almada and Edgar

Mengual Herken to three years. The Attorney General's Office stated the courts overcame 1,200 motions presented by defense attorneys to arrive at the sentences.

<u>Financial Disclosure</u>: The constitution requires all public employees, including elected officials and employees of independent government entities, to disclose their income and assets within 15 days of taking office or receiving an appointment and again within 15 days of finishing their term or assignment. Public employees must also disclose assets and income of spouses and dependent children.

The law mandates the Comptroller's Office monitor and verify disclosures; the Comptroller may make income and asset disclosures public only at the request of the executive branch, congress, the Attorney General's Office, or judicial authorities. The Attorney General's Office opened several investigations for inconsistencies related to these disclosures.

The law bars public employees from holding government positions for up to 10 years for failure to comply with financial disclosure laws and imposes monetary fines of up to Gs. 19.1 million ($3,350), but this was generally not enforced. Filings often were late, incomplete, or misleading, and many simply did not disclose their finances. Legislators generally ignored the law with impunity, using political immunity to avoid investigation or prosecution.

<u>Public Access to Information</u>: The constitution guarantees public access to government information. Citizens and noncitizens, including foreign media representatives, had access to government information.

From January 1 to September 1, the Public Access to Information Unit in the Ministry of Justice received and responded to 1,162 requests for information. Since the access to information law entered into force in 2015, more than 80 public offices, from all branches and levels of government, have opened an office to receive and manage information requests. The executive branch, through the Ministry of Justice and the Secretariat for Information and Communication Technology, created a "one-stop-shopping" website for citizens to file information requests and find data pertaining to other requests. The website provides statistics and infographics on the number of requests filed by month, by public office, and by location. As of September 1, the website has processed over 2,100 requests.

Section 5. Governmental Attitude Regarding International and Nongovernmental Investigation of Alleged Violations of Human Rights

More than 50 domestic and international human rights groups operated, generally without government restriction, investigating and publishing their findings on human rights cases. Government officials generally cooperated with domestic NGOs and international organizations and met with domestic NGO monitors and representatives, but often did not take action in response to their reports or recommendations. The government has responded to recommendations of international bodies and international NGOs.

<u>Government Human Rights Bodies</u>: On November 1, the Chamber of Deputies approved Miguel Godoy Servin and Carlos Vera Bordaberry as Human Rights Ombudsman and Assistant Ombudsman, respectively, the country's two primary human rights advocates. Servin replaced Manuel Paez Monges, whose term expired in 2006. Monges continued to serve because the Chamber of Deputies did not vote for a replacement. Human rights organizations, victims of the Stroessner dictatorship, and several congressional members strongly criticized the previous Ombudsman for what they considered ineffective and negligent handling of human rights advocacy. The office lacked independence, published no reports during the year, and has not issued an annual report to Congress on human rights since 2005.

The Senate and Chamber of Deputies Committees on Human Rights made frequent fact-finding trips within the country, including visits to several prisons, ruled on legislative proposals pertaining to human rights, issued occasional reports, and responded to constituent inquiries about human rights problems.

The NMPT has the legal prerogative to visit and inspect, without judicial authorization, any prison, police station, military installation, children's shelter, and retirement home. An inter-institutional commission composed of representatives from the three government branches and civil society selects NMPT commissioners. During the year, the NMPT made several inspection visits and participated in public hearings on hazing against military cadets.

Several human rights NGOs, including Amnesty International and CODEHUPY, complained there is no single, reliable point of contact within the Paraguayan government to discuss human rights issues. They stated they were not approached for consultations on human rights policies, planning, and legislation. Although several government ministries had human rights offices to monitor compliance with human rights legislation, there was no coordinator to serve as the point of contact with civil society. The Justice Ministry withdrew a draft law elevating its Human Rights Office to the vice-minister level despite assurances at the beginning of the year to follow through. The office would coordinate with all executive branch human rights offices and be responsible for the implementation of the National Plan for Human Rights.

Section 6. Discrimination, Societal Abuses, and Trafficking in Persons

Women

Rape and Domestic Violence: The law criminalizes rape, including spousal rape, and provides penalties of up to 10 years in prison for rape or sexual assault. If the victim is a minor, the sentence ranges from a minimum of three years to 15 years in prison. According to the Attorney General's office, rape continued to be a significant and pervasive problem. The government generally prosecuted rape allegations and sometimes obtained convictions; however, it is believed many rapes went unreported due to fear of stigma or retribution. The Attorney General's office lacked a specialized unit for cases of gender violence and abuse of children and adolescents. The specialized unit for human trafficking and commercial sexual exploitation of children of the Attorney General's office was sometimes assigned cases, but it lacked sufficient resources to pursue them. Police generally did not prioritize reports of rape.

As of September, the Attorney General's Office received 736 complaints of rape. The National Police reported receiving 543 rape complaints from January to July, of which they detained 307 alleged perpetrators. Victims often filed complaints with different institutions, depending on their level of trust in that institution.

Although the law criminalizes domestic violence, including psychological abuse, and stipulates a penalty of two years in prison or a fine if convicted, it requires the abuse to be habitual and the aggressor and victim to be "cohabitating or lodging together." Judges typically issued fines, but in some cases they sentenced offenders to jail to provide for the safety of the victim. Despite increased reports of domestic violence, individuals often withdrew complaints soon after filing due to spousal reconciliation or family pressure. In some instances, the courts mediated domestic violence cases. According to NGOs and the Ministry of Women's Affairs, domestic violence was widespread, and thousands of women received treatment for injuries sustained in domestic altercations. The Ministry of Women's Affairs promoted the national 24-hour telephone hotline for domestic abuse victims. The ministry offers domestic violence victims information, counseling, and psychological and legal support.

The Ministry of Women's Affairs operated a shelter for female victims of trafficking or domestic violence in Asuncion. The ministry also coordinated victim assistance efforts, public outreach campaigns, and training with the National Police and healthcare units. The ministry, the Attorney General's Office, and various NGOs provided health and psychological assistance, including shelter, to victims. The ministry also provided victims assistance courses for police, healthcare workers, and prosecutors.

The National Police has 16 specialized units to attend victims of domestic violence and 118 officers are assigned to these stations. As of August 31, the National Police reported 7,165 complaints of domestic violence, and its Unit for Intra-Family Violence assisted 4,060 victims.

Sexual Harassment: The law prohibits sexual harassment and stipulates a penalty of two years in prison or a fine; however, sexual harassment remained a widespread problem for many women, especially in workplace environments. Prosecutors found sexual harassment and abuse claims difficult to prove because of victims' fear of workplace retaliation and societal pressures against victims. Many dropped their complaints or were unwilling to continue cooperating with prosecutors. As of August 31, the National Police reported receiving 16 complaints of sexual harassment.

Reproductive Rights: Couples and individuals have the right to decide the number, spacing, and timing of their children; manage their reproductive health; and have access to the information and means to do so, free from discrimination, coercion, or violence. Reproductive health services were concentrated in cities, and rural areas faced significant gaps in coverage. According to United Nations Population Fund estimates, adolescent birth rate remains high, at 63 per 1,000 women aged 15-19 in 2015. In 2015 UNICEF reported that two girls between the ages of 10 and 14 give birth every day in the country.

According to the World Health Organization (WHO), maternal mortality is high with an estimated 132 deaths per 100,000 live births. WHO notes the risk of maternal death is four times higher among girls under 16 than among women in their 20s. Abortion is explicitly permitted if the mother's life is deemed at risk.

Discrimination: The constitution prohibits discrimination based on sex, but the government did not effectively enforce these provisions. There is no comprehensive law against discrimination, thus no legal basis for enforcement of the constitutional clause against discrimination.

Women generally enjoyed the same legal status and rights as men. Nonetheless, gender-related discrimination was widespread. Women experienced more difficulty than men in securing employment and occupation (see section 7.d.). Women generally obtained employment as domestic workers, secretaries, sales staff, and customer service representatives.

Children

Birth Registration: Nationality derives from birth within the country's territory, from birth to government employees in service abroad, or from birth to a citizen residing temporarily outside the country. Hospitals immediately register births. Citizenship conveys to all nationals who attain the age of 18 as well as to older persons upon naturalization. Birth certificates and national identity documents are a prerequisite to access government services, including obtaining a passport.

Education: Education is free, compulsory, and universal from kindergarten through secondary school. According to the government, girls from rural families tended to leave school at a younger age than did boys. Approximately 10 percent of children from poor families did not have access to schooling, due to economic hardship, geographic isolation, or early entrance into the workforce.

Child Abuse: The NGO Coalition for the Rights of Children and Adolescents and the Secretariat of Children and Adolescents (SNNA) stated that violence against children was widespread and equally prevalent among rural and urban families. As of September 30, the Attorney General's Office reported 596 cases of child abuse (compared to 973 cases in all of 2015) and 295 cases of rape of minors (compared to 491 cases in 2015).

There were no government shelters for abused children. Local Catholic charities operated several children's homes and orphanages. In many cities the municipal council for children's rights assisted abused and neglected children.

According to the SNNA and the NMPT, there were approximately 60 private children's shelters housing more than 2,000 children.

Early and Forced Marriage: The government increased the minimum legal age for marriage from 16 to 18 through a law published in May 2015. The law permits marriage for those aged 16 to 18 with parental consent, and for those younger than age 16 only with judicial authorization under exceptional circumstances. There were no reports of forced marriage.

Sexual Exploitation of Children: According to the SNNA, exploitation of children in prostitution or forced domestic service remained problematic. The law provides penalties of up to eight years of imprisonment for persons responsible for pimping or brokering victims younger than 17 years.

The minimum age of consent is 14 when married and 16 when not married. While there is a statutory rape law for those under 14, the maximum penalty is a fine for opposite-sex partners and prison for same-sex partners. The law was not effectively enforced. The penal code prohibits the production, distribution, and possession of pornography involving children or adolescents younger than age 18. Production of pornographic images of children may result in a fine or up to three years in prison. Authorities may increase this penalty to 10 years in prison depending on the age of the child and the child's relationship to the abuser.

As of September 30, the Attorney General's office reported 1,299 cases of sexual abuse against children, compared with 2,196 cases in 2015.

For non-intercourse sexual abuse of a minor, the maximum sentence is up to three years or a fine. For cases involving intercourse, authorities can increase the sentence to 10 years. As of September 30, the Attorney General's Office received 295 complaints of rape of minors (compared to 491 cases in 2015).

Child Soldiers: The government as well as NGOs, including the Coordinator for the Rights of Infants and Adolescents and the Peace and Justice Service, alleged that EPP and ACA continued recruitment of children, most of whom reportedly were relatives of adult EPP and ACA members. The children started in logistical support roles, carrying supplies to members in the field and serving as lookouts, before later being incorporated as full-time combatants, usually between 14 and 16 years of age.

Institutionalized Children: The NMPT and the SNNA both have the responsibility and mandate to visit and inspect children's shelters and ensure the well-being of institutionalized children. They both regularly made recommendations to close shelters.

An NMPT report on a June 5 inspection of the privately run Gotitas de Amor shelter in Ita, Central Department, highlighted deplorable conditions, with boys and girls residing together without adult supervision. According to the report, children lacked identity documents, and many did not attend school. The NMPT subsequently reported their findings to other state agencies to remedy the situation and move children to foster families.

International Child Abductions: The country is a party to the 1980 Hague Convention on the Civil Aspects of International Child Abduction. See the Department of State's *Annual Report on International Parental Child Abduction* at travel.state.gov/content/childabduction/en/legal/compliance.html.

Anti-Semitism

The Jewish community has fewer than 1,000 members. There were no reports of anti-Semitic acts.

Trafficking in Persons

See the Department of State's Trafficking in Persons Report at www.state.gov/j/tip/rls/tiprpt/.

Persons with Disabilities

The law nominally prohibits discrimination against persons with physical, sensory, intellectual, and mental disabilities in employment, education, public transportation, access to health care, the judicial system, or the provision of other state services. The law generally does not mandate accessibility for persons with disabilities, and most of the country's buildings remained inaccessible, though some municipalities made minor progress.

Many persons with disabilities faced significant discrimination in employment; others were unable to seek employment because of a lack of accessible public transportation. The law mandates the allocation of five percent of all available public employee positions, approximately 10,000 positions, to persons with disabilities. In 2016, government employees with disabilities constituted less than one percent of public-sector employees. The Ministry of Education estimated more than 50 percent of children with disabilities did not attend school because of lack of access to public transportation.

The National Secretariat for the Rights of Persons with Disabilities is responsible for certifying disability status. No law specifically provides for access to information or communications.

National/Racial/Ethnic Minorities

Anecdotally, ethnic minorities reported discrimination in such areas as employment, credit, pay, owning and/or managing businesses, education, and housing.

Indigenous People

The law provides indigenous persons the right to participate in the economic, social, political, and cultural life of the country, but the law was not effectively enforced. Discrimination, coupled with a lack of access to employment, education, health care, shelter, and sufficient land, hindered the ability of indigenous persons to progress economically while maintaining their cultural identity (see section 7.d.). The government does not discriminate in the type of legal status or recognition it gives to each indigenous group.

Indigenous populations comprised a higher percentage of the population within the Chaco region, and communities there had more difficulty accessing government and judicial services and faced more severe political and economic exclusion.

Indigenous workers engaged as laborers on ranches typically earned low wages, worked long hours, received pay infrequently or not at all, and lacked medical or retirement benefits. This situation was particularly severe in the Chaco region.

The National Institute for Indigenous Affairs (INDI), the Attorney General's office, Justice Ministry, Labor Ministry, the Social Action Secretariat, and the Ombudsman's office are responsible for protecting and promoting indigenous rights. The law mandates that INDI negotiate, purchase, and register land on behalf of indigenous communities who claim lack of access to their ancestral lands. In some instances INDI claimed it lacked sufficient funding to purchase land on behalf of indigenous persons and/or required them to register land in Asuncion rather than locally.

The law authorizes indigenous persons to determine how to use communal land. In some cases indigenous citizens transferred or rented community land to nonindigenous persons, who illegally harvested fish or cleared land to cultivate crops. There were also several reported cases of illegal deforestation of indigenous lands for charcoal production and cattle ranching. There were insufficient police and judicial protections from encroachments on indigenous lands. This often resulted in conflict between indigenous communities and large landowners in rural areas, which at times led to violence.

CODEHUPY and other NGOs documented widespread trafficking in persons, rape, sexual harassment, and physical abuse of women in indigenous communities. Perpetrators were often neighboring workers and employers from ranches and farms.

During the year CODEHUPY alleged that rural landowners, acting in complicity with local authorities and security forces, harassed landless peasant groups, indigenous tribes, and land-reform activists.

On September 30, police forcibly evicted the Ava Guarani indigenous community from 1,047 hectares of ancestral land in Sauce, near Minga Pora, Alto Parana Department. CODEHUPY reported the police demolished and burned down homes, schools, places of worship, and crops, as well as stole domestic animals. CODEHUPY alleged German Hutz, the owner of adjacent agricultural land, leveraged his ties to Vice President Juan Afara to obtain a court order for the eviction. The community lobbied for the removal of Aldo Saldivar, head of INDI, for annulling a 2013 resolution stating the government owed a debt for relocating certain indigenous communities, including the Ava Guarani, during the construction of the Itaipu Dam.

On July 11, the government finalized the documents and made the first down payment to purchase land for the Xakmok Kasek indigenous community per a 2000 ruling by the Inter-American Court on Human Rights (IACHR).

On February 3, the IACHR formally requested the government adopt precautionary measures in favor of the rights of the Ayoreo Totobiegosode People, especially of the communities in voluntary isolation, known as the Jonoine-Urasade. The request was based on allegations that local cattle ranchers had conducted a series of intrusions onto and deforestation activities on their land.

Acts of Violence, Discrimination, and Other Abuses Based on Sexual Orientation and Gender Identity

No laws explicitly prohibit discrimination against LGBTI persons in employment, housing, access to education, or health care; all types of such discrimination, including societal discrimination, occurred frequently. Penalties for sex with a minor between ages 14 and 16 are more severe if the victim and perpetrator are of the same sex. Same-sex perpetrators are subject to up to two years in prison; the maximum penalty for opposite-sex perpetrators is a fine. CODEHUPY reported widespread police harassment and discrimination against LGBTI persons (see section 7 d.).

According to reports, police officers regularly beat, robbed, and implicated transgender individuals as suspects in serious crimes, including drug trafficking and armed robbery. NGOs alleged transgender individuals were forced to work in the sex trade because of discrimination and lack of employment options.

HIV and AIDS Social Stigma

The law prohibits discrimination based on HIV-positive status and protects the privacy of medical information. The law also specifically prohibits employers from discriminating against or harassing employees based on their HIV-positive status. Labor Ministry regulations forbid employers from requiring HIV testing prior to employment, but many companies still did so.

CODEHUPY noted that persons with HIV/AIDS faced discrimination as well as societal intimidation in health care, education, and employment based on their sexual orientation, serological state, demand for HIV testing, or gender identity. The NGO referred complaints to the Attorney General's Office and National Police for investigation. The center also established hotlines to receive complaints.

Section 7. Worker Rights

a. Freedom of Association and the Right to Collective Bargaining

The law, including related regulations and statutory instruments, provides for the right of workers to form and join independent unions (with the exception of the armed forces and police), bargain collectively, and conduct legal strikes. The law prohibits binding arbitration or retribution against union organizers and strikers. There are several restrictions on these rights. The law requires that industrial unions have a minimum of 300 members to register; that is excessive by international standards. All unions must register with the Labor Ministry, a process that often takes more than a year. The ministry, however, typically issued provisional registrations within weeks of application to allow labor unions to operate. Unions with provisional registrations had the same rights and obligations as other unions. Workers cannot be members of more than one union, even if they have more than one part-time employment contract. Strikes are limited to purposes directly linked to workers' occupations. Candidates for trade union office must work for a company and be active members of the union.

The Labor Ministry is responsible for enforcing labor rights, registering unions, mediating disputes, and overseeing social security and retirement programs. Penalties, fines, and remedies associated with discrimination against unions were generally ineffective. Investigations of anti-union discrimination to protect labor rights were rare, lacked sufficient resources, and reportedly occurred only if requested by an aggrieved party. The ministry does not have jurisdiction to initiate or participate in anti-union litigation. Employers who fail to recognize or work collectively to bargain with a registered union face fines of 50 days' wages, or approximately Gs. 3.5 million ($636). Employers who blacklist employees face fines of only 30 days' wages, or approximately Gs. 2.1 million ($382). These penalties were not sufficient to deter violations. The government often did not prevent retaliation by employers who took action against strikers and union leaders. Administrative and judicial procedures were subject to lengthy delays, mishandling of cases, and corruption.

The government did not always respect unions' freedom of association and the right to collectively bargain. Employers' associations heavily influenced some private-sector unions. The leadership of several unions representing public-sector employees had ties to political parties and the government.

While union workers from the steel and maritime industries were unionized and often received relevant legal protections, most workers, including farmers, ranchers, and informal-sector employees, did not participate in labor unions. Many of these workers were members of farm-worker movements. Unlike the previous year, there were no reports of civil disobedience to extract payments or to demand reparations.

b. Prohibition of Forced or Compulsory Labor

The law prohibits all forms of forced or compulsory labor. The government did not effectively enforce the law. The Labor Ministry lacked adequate resources to conduct inspections, especially in remote areas where forced labor was reportedly more prevalent. Penalties for violations include up to 20 years in prison. Minimal enforcement and penalties were insufficient to deter violations.

NGOs, indigenous organizations, the Central Workers Unit, and the International Labor Organization filed formal complaints on behalf of indigenous workers in the Chaco region working under forced labor, specifically debt-bondage conditions. Workers did not receive pay, received pay in kind with substandard food items, or were forced to purchase goods at debt-inducing prices at a company store. There were also press reports that drug trafficking organizations in Amambay, Canindeyu, San Pedro, and Concepcion Departments recruited workers into forced labor to process marijuana.

During the year, the Labor Ministry's regional office in the Chaco received some complaints for unjustified firings, nonpayment of wages, and other labor violations. The ministry did not confirm instances of debt bondage in the Chaco, but would not dismiss the possibility that it continued to exist. The government continued anti-trafficking law enforcement and training efforts and provided limited protective services to female and child trafficking victims.

Forced child labor, particularly in domestic service, was a significant problem (see section 7.c.). Reports of "criadazgo" continued throughout the year. "Criadazgo" is the practice where middle and upper income families informally "employ" young domestic workers, often from impoverished families, and provide them with shelter, food, some education, and a small stipend.

See the Department of State's annual Trafficking in Persons Report at www.state.gov/j/tip/rls/tiprpt.

c. Prohibition of Child Labor and Minimum Age for Employment

The minimum age for full-time employment is 18. Children 14 to 18 years old may work if they have a written authorization from their parents, attend school, do not work more than four hours a day, and do not work more than a maximum of 24 hours per week. The law also permits "light work" for children between the ages of 12 and 14.

The maximum administrative penalty for employing a child under age 14 is Gs. 3.78 million ($687). The law stipulates those who employ adolescents between ages14 and 18 under hazardous conditions must pay the maximum administrative penalty and/or three to five years in prison, but the penalties were insufficient to deter violations.

The government did not effectively enforce laws protecting children from exploitation in the workplace. The Labor Ministry is responsible for enforcing child labor laws and the Attorney General's office prosecutes violators. The Ombudsman's office and the Child Rights Committee receive complaints and refer them to the Attorney General's office. As of September 30, the Labor Ministry received 17 complaints regarding child and adolescent workers. Of the 17 complaints, 12 were for boys and five for girls. Most worked as metalworkers, cashiers, sales clerks, helpers, and in other service jobs. In 2015, the Labor Ministry received 20 complaints from child and adolescent workers.

The National Commission for the Prevention and Eradication of Child Labor worked to eliminate exploitative child labor by increasing awareness, improving legal protections and public policy, and implementing monitoring systems, but resource constraints limited the effectiveness of these efforts. Child labor continued to be a problem in sugar, brick, and limestone manufacturing, domestic service, and agricultural sectors. Children, primarily boys, also worked in the manufacturing and agricultural sectors and in the restaurant and other service industries. Children also worked as vendors in markets. According to UNICEF and the SNNA, an estimated 46,000 children, primarily girls, worked as domestic servants and received no pay. In exchange for work, employers promised child domestic servants room, board, and financial support for school. Some of these children were victims of forced child labor, did not receive pay or the promised benefits in exchange for work, suffered from sexual exploitation, and often lacked access to education.

On January 20, Tomas Eligio Ferreiro Rojas, a retired military official, allegedly killed 14-year old Carolina Marin after repeatedly striking her with a tree limb in Vaqueria, Caazapa. Ferreiro Rojas and his common-law wife, Ramona Triflacion Melgarejo Figueredo (an employee at the Public Registry), were the legal guardians of Carolina Ruiz, but employed her as a domestic servant. The Attorney General's office charged Ferreiro Rojas and Melgarejo with aggravated murder, domestic violence, and violation of the duty to protect a child. The case was pending as of November 1.

The worst forms of child labor occurred where malnourished, abused, or neglected children worked in unhealthy and hazardous conditions selling goods or services on the street, working in factories, or harvesting crops. Children were used, procured, and offered to third parties for illicit activities, including commercial sexual exploitation (see also section 6, Children), sometimes with the knowledge of parents and guardians, who received remuneration. Some minors were coerced into acting as drug smugglers along the border with Brazil as part of criminal syndicates. There were also reports of child and adolescent soldiers with the EPP.

See the Department of Labor's Findings on the Worst Forms of Child Labor at www.dol.gov/ilab/reports/child-labor/findings/.

d. Discrimination with Respect to Employment or Occupation

The labor code specifically prohibits discrimination based on race, color, sex, age, religion, political opinion, or social origin. Other legislation prohibits discrimination based on disability and HIV-positive status. Laws and regulations mandate that five percent of public employees be persons with disabilities. These laws and regulations were often not enforced. No specific legislation forbids labor discrimination based on national origin, citizenship, sexual orientation, gender identity, language, or having a communicable disease.

The government did not effectively enforce applicable law and penalties were insufficient to deter violations. According to Article 385 of the Paraguayan Labor Code, the fines for discrimination range from 10 to 30 daily wages per affected worker. Fines are doubled for multiple offenses.

The press reported on employment discrimination based on sex, race, disability, age, language, weight, sexual orientation, HIV-positive status, and pregnancy. On May 3, the NGO Center for HIV-AIDS Discrimination Complaints reported receiving dozens of complaints since 2012 of companies screening job applicants and dismissing employees with positive test results for HIV-AIDs. They also reported employers forcing employees with HIV-AIDs to use separate restrooms.

In order to raise awareness of discrimination in the workplace, the Labor Ministry organized three career fairs for job applicants over the age of 40, applicants with disabilities, applicants with adverse credit histories, and applicants from indigenous communities.

e. Acceptable Conditions of Work

The mandatory national minimum wage is approximately Gs. 1.8 million ($327) per month. According to a study in 2015 conducted by the General Directorate for

Statistics (DGEEC) and the Economic and Social Development Planning Secretariat, the average per capita monthly income was approximately Gs. 1,934,166 ($351). Per the same report, the poverty income level varied from Gs. 396,266 ($72) per month in rural areas to Gs. 643,606 ($117) per month in metropolitan Asuncion, and the extreme poverty income level ranged from Gs. 268,794 ($49) per month in rural areas to Gs. 378,520 ($69) per month in metropolitan Asuncion.

By law, domestic workers must receive 60 percent of the minimum wage (Gs.1,094,433, or $198), and housing and food count toward a domestic worker's salary. The law stipulates that domestic employees work a maximum of eight hours per day, are entitled to overtime if they exceed these hours, and have the right to enjoy a weekly rest of 36 hours, as well as all national holidays paid. The law provides for a standard legal workweek of 48 hours (42 hours for night work) with one and one-half days of rest. The law also mandates payment of at least one annual bonus of one month's salary and a minimum of 12 days' and a maximum of 30 days' vacation per year, depending on total years of service. There are no prohibitions of, or exceptions for, excessive compulsory overtime.

Per the Labor Ministry and NGOs, many domestic workers suffered discrimination, routinely worked 12-hour workdays, were not paid for overtime work, were allowed to rest less than the minimum time allowed by law, were not entitled to publicly provided retirement benefits, and did not routinely attain job stability after 10 years, unlike other workers covered by the labor code. Domestic workers were eligible for government-sponsored medical care and retirement programs through small payroll and employer contributions.

The government sets appropriate occupational health and safety standards stipulating conditions of safety, hygiene, and comfort. Although these standards were current and appropriate for light-manufacturing and construction industries, enforcement was inadequate.

The Labor Ministry did not effectively enforce provisions for overtime pay, the minimum wage, or limitations on hours of work in the formal or the informal sector. It launched public awareness campaigns, however, aimed at employers to remind them of their labor obligations.

As of September 9, the Labor Ministry's Department of Mediation of Private Conflicts received 5,571 labor complaints and mediation requests. Men filed the majority of these complaints, which involved illegal dismissals or the failure of employers to pay the legally mandated end-of-year bonuses. DGEEC estimated the percentage of workers who received the minimum wage or more, increased from 71.1 percent in 2015 to 73.7 percent in the second semester of 2016. Many formal and informal employers violated provisions requiring overtime pay, particularly in the food and agricultural sectors and for domestic services. From January to September 31, the Labor Ministry received 100 complaints of occupational safety and health violations, some associated with workplace accidents or fatalities. Most workplace accidents or fatalities occurred in the construction and light-manufacturing industries.

On February 23, the Attorney General's Office charged and ordered the arrest of Gustavo Perez Codas, owner of a leather-tanning factory in San Antonio, for the death of two workers who died in a workplace accident. The case was pending at year's end.

Employers are obligated to register workers with the Labor Ministry. As of September 30, however, approximately 2,157 employers had registered a total of 7,091 workers with the Labor Ministry, a low number compared to the country's population of approximately 6.6 million. The UN Development Program's 2013 Human Development and Social Security study concluded 81.3 percent of the labor force (2,371,000) worked in informal jobs and did not receive labor law protections.

Paraguay considers the informal economy to be any economic activities performed by persons not registered under the laws governing tax, employment, and social security. In some cases, workers received a formal salary, of which they and their employers paid social security tax, and an additional, undeclared salary. Some businesses were formally registered to operate and pay taxes, but they did not register or declare their entire staff to the employment authorities.